The English Strain

Also by Robert Sheppard (* published by Shearsman Books)

Poetry
Returns
Daylight Robbery
The Flashlight Sonata
Transit Depots/Empty Diaries (with John Seed [text] and Patricia Farrell [images])
Empty Diaries
The Lores
The Anti-Orpheus: a notebook *
Tin Pan Arcadia
Hymns to the God in which My Typewriter Believes
Complete Twentieth Century Blues
Warrant Error *
Berlin Bursts *
The Given
A Translated Man *
Words Out of Time
Unfinish
History or Sleep — Selected Poems *
Twitters for a Lark (co-authored) *
Micro Event Space
Bad Idea

Fiction
The Only Life

Edited
Floating Capital: New Poets from London (with Adrian Clarke)
News for the Ear: A Homage to Roy Fisher (with Peter Robinson)
The Salt Companion to Lee Harwood
The Door at Taldir: Selected Poems of Paul Evans *
Atlantic Drift: an anthology of poetry and poetics (with James Byrne)

Criticism
Far Language: Poetics and Linguistically Innovative Poetry 1978–1997
The Poetry of Saying: British Poetry and Its Discontents 1950–2000
Iain Sinclair
When Bad Times Made for Good Poetry *
The Meaning of Form in Contemporary Innovative Poetry

On Robert Sheppard
The Robert Sheppard Companion, ed. Byrne & Madden *

Robert Sheppard

The English Strain

Shearsman Books

First published in the United Kingdom in 2021 by
Shearsman Books Ltd
PO Box 4239
Swindon
SN3 9FN

Shearsman Books Ltd Registered Office
30–31 St. James Place, Mangotsfield, Bristol BS16 9JB
(this address not for correspondence)

www.shearsman.com

ISBN 978-1-84861-746-9

Copyright © Robert Sheppard, 2021.

The right of Robert Sheppard to be identified as the author
of this work has been asserted by him in accordance with the
Copyrights, Designs and Patents Act of 1988.
All rights reserved.

Contents

Petrarch 3 – a derivative dérive	7
Overdubs	27
Mayan Thoughts at Brighton	34
New Ghost	35
It's Nothing	37
Breakout	53
Hap: Understudies of Thomas Wyatt's Petrarch	
Perhaps a Mishap	63
Hap 1–15	64
Hap Hazard	79
Surrey with the Fringe on Top	
The Unfortunate Fellow Traveller	83
Direct Rule	90
Elegaic Sonnets	
Petrarch of Petworth: the Earl of Sussex	97
The South Downs Way	103
Non-Disclosure Agreement	
Brazilian Sonnets	117
Cake and Eat it Britain	124
Acknowledgements	132
Note	133
Selected Resources	134

My verse is the true image of my Mind,
   Ever in motion, still desiring change;
And as thus to varietie inclin'd,
   So in all Humors sportively I range:
     My muse is rightly of the English straine,
     That cannot long one fashion intertaine.
         —Michael Drayton

Petrarch 3

a derivative dérive

for the Petrarch Boys
Tim Atkins and Peter Hughes

and in homage to
Nicholas Moore and Harry Mathews

Era il giorno ch'al sol si scoloraro
per la pietà del suo factore i rai,
quando i' fui preso, et non me ne guardai,
ché i be' vostr'occhi, donna, mi legaro.

Tempo non mi parea da far riparo
contra colpi d'Amor: però m'andai
secur, senza sospetto; onde i miei guai
nel commune dolor s'incominciaro.

Trovommi Amor del tutto disarmato
et aperta la via per gli occhi al core,
che di lagrime son fatti uscio et varco:

però al mio parer, non li fu honore
ferir me de saetta in quello stato,
a voi armata non mostrar pur l'arco.

Era il giorno ch'al sol si scoloraro

That pitiful morning when the light of Heaven
Was hidden for our mourning maker's sake,
I saw you first that day, My Lady, but
Was captured, disarmed, then bound to your stake.

It didn't seem the time for shields and armour
Against Love's arrows, his batters and blows;
So, unsuspecting, I wept with the world,
But that day my heartbreaks began, my woes.

Love stalked me, found me, unarmed and weak,
And opened my eyes, portals of tears, through which
Sorrow flowed from the passage of my heart.

But feeble was Love's triumph to triumph
With his arrow over one so enfeebled,
And to not even dare to flash you his dart.

Iron Maiden

Latex skies. Low cloud obscuring celestial
domination. I clapped my fuck-eye on you,
which you then pierced on a glance, that day,
and dragged me naked to your torture chamber.

The funeral of Thatcher seemed the right time
for your whip and irons. Posties brushed up their
MaggieMaggieMaggie chants and I cried *onions-
onions-onions*, stinging eyes fixed on your heels.

You stalked me in your lace-up stockings, striding tight,
and took my tears for real pain, yet can't you see desire
burning under the dildo mask you've clamped on my kisser?

Easy prey for your domination, bitch! Slap!
I crumple to the floor. Would rubbery Love
through his pouch dare to flash you his horn?

Pet

Up at dawn (though it was the Shortest Day),
He was nursing a Mad Friday hangover,
But took me on walkies to Seffie. He took a selfie
By the Palm House. Tied to the gate I first saw you.

It was Brass Monkeys, believe me. Licking my bollocks
Was like snuffling dropped ice cream dollops;
The men in their flashing Santa hats looked lugubrious
But the depth of my despair exceeded their Christmas Blues!

Your wet nose sniffled my arse and I growled and howled
Like a stud-dog. I slobbered and chafed at my chains.
He kicked me and my jaws locked on my bilious yelp.

You lifted your tail like a poodle, fluffy tart,
Tripping past my flailing mass of muscle and lust.
He didn't even notice, phone in hand, boot in my nuts.

Petrak: the first English sonnet, Good Friday 1401

The morwe biganne when hevene its bemes
In routhe of our Lord hid al the lighte.
My Lady I espeyde, she rent al my dremes,
This wight bounden to wommens tendre myghte.

It was nat the tyme for speres sharp and stronge
Agan arwes of Love and his strook and smoot.
Withouten sheeldes or defence I wep ful longe
swich a love-longyne's desperaunce, as I woot.

Love cam russhyng to smerte my peynes sorwe
Fro the breething prisoun of my distempre hert,
To open myn eyen and resolven the flo.

Love's dominacion is yet deedly narwe
Yif I am so wrecche, wounden bi a dart
Whil you, unbuxomnesse Lady, escap his bow.

A Florentine Vampire in Paris

Amid the rush of All Souls' Eve, the majesty of sadness
(I'd waited 530 years for this translation, this transfusion)
a woman mourned, passing slowly, lifted by the liquefaction
of her clothes; holding fast the stake to my bloated heart.

Like a wobbling lush, not feeling blows or blood,
Under a livid sky of germs I fed off her grace,
statuesque. I wept, drank deep from her softening eyes.
Fascination weakens. Pain kills: pleasure bites.

I've paid in blood but not my own, nor my words.
Love flashed and she flooded, ensanguined and weak:
bleak eternity escaped into the void vessel of her heart.

Ever! There's no living beat in this unloving verse:
O you whom I might have loved if I'd dared not to
flash you my fangs! O you who'd read it all before!

Semantic Poetry Translation

to the memory of Stefan Themerson

In that first part of the day
    holding all that can be contained
    having copious feeling for the sufferings
    and misfortunes of others
        when the agency by which objects are rendered visible
        by electromagnetic radiation
        capable of producing visual sensation
    in the vault of sky overhanging the earth
    the dwelling place of God
                or the gods and the blessèd
                    was concealed
              on account
              of the one who makes
    namely the Creator
    who murmured in a sorrowful manner
    as in grief
I perceived by the sense seated in the eye
you
    for the foremost occasion regarded as
one of a number of multiplied instances in a recurring series
on that particular holy time
    the anniversary of the death of the son of God
that the earth takes to revolve on its axis
    O woman of refined manners and instincts
    of chivalric devotion
            belonging to me
but I was taken by force as a prize
stripped of armour
rendered defenceless
        deprived of the power of hurt
   before being
   restrained
   then
   fastened with a band
to your post to which one condemned to be burned is tied

It did not appear to be
the moment at which to entertain
                broad plates carried to ward off weapons
and defensive dress
        to protect me from straight pointed missiles
        made to be shot from a bow
                or beatings with successive blows
                or strokes or knocks
belonging to or pertaining to or deriving from
the devoted affection or sexual love for someone
(else)
or the personification of
                the devoted affection
or sexual love for someone (else)
        as the deity
        of the devoted affection or sexual love for someone
        (else)
                namely Cupid or Eros
so
having no inclination to believe without sufficient evidence
        I lamented
        by leaking
        drops of liquid secreted by the lachrymal gland
        in concordance with
                the system of things which accommodates
                the inhabitants of this universe
but at that moment of existence
the crushing sorrows or miseries
that belong to myself alone
arose
and came into being

Eros or Cupid came after me
keeping under cover
succeeded in tracking down
        me
        who was not furnished with means of protection

    who was wanting strength
            or mental
            or moral
            or artistic
                      force
and he exposed the interior of my organ of sight
or vision
its great gate or magnificent
egress
for
drops of liquid secreted by the lachrymal gland
from end to end
    as abundant pain of mind
    seeped
    from the
    transitional tubes
    of the imagined seat of my affections

But
the exultation at the success
of the deity of the devoted affection
or sexual love for someone
(else) was
        forceless
            vacillating
                faint
    in its celebration of victory with pomp
    not even bold enough to venture
    to make show in a blaze of brilliant sparkles
        of his pointed weapon
        or toy
        for throwing with the hand
or of a calcareous needle supposed to be used
    as a sexual stimulus
        by snails

twittersonnet

after René Van Valckenborch

dark morn
sad god/sa
w you/stak
ed me/bad

time for l
ove's blow
/wept woe/
stalked my

heart pou
rs/weak Er
os struck

weak-me/no
guts to s
how a dart

Pale

for Peter Manson

Tonight, I don't come to capture your body
bearing my sins for the sake of the world; or,
my Beast, to tear up a pitiful storm in your fuzz,
from the incurable *ennui* I drop with the kiss of my verse;

I demand of your bed dreamless sleep armoured against
crepuscular amours, clouded in the curtains of unknowing;
so you'll taste your own black lies, the batters and blues,
you who know more about *le néant* than the dead.

Le Vice stalked me, gobbled me, sucked out my grace;
impaled, like you, sterile tears unflowing,
while your stone breast is dressed to kill whose

heart no glistening fang of crime unblesses,
I run, run down, haunted by my shroud,
afraid of dying in my sleep, in the poem, alone.

Empty Diary 1327

His eye is pulled to the black hole
at the centre of my white body. It's the reason
I'm here this morning, snarling under my wimple,
snapping this backward dilation as a trap.

His dream has made his eye into a ball.
His moist balls turn to weeping eyes
for this singular event, his wordy woe.
The Devil's tunes are pitched in pitch:

incantations soften the pink gash pushed out
in the middle of my bending, *L'Origine
du Monde* reprised. Sorrow seeps from his pump.

Into Hell's jaws I cast the flapper and the slapper.
Trust a Florentine not to have seen where the fault lay:
the strung-up Megalomaniac rapping in riddles.

Now then now then then and now

God's not too pleased with me. For his sake (and mine)
don't tell the Duchess! That's why you caught me
running the Marathon each year, raising shekels by the shedload,
while I jogged into my next faceless wrap of baby-flab.

In my time I spun the grooves and groped the grubs
from the milk bars of Leeds to the morgue at Broadmoor,
consummate in the toilets of Broadcasting House. Now
then: hate is when you're feeling Top of the Pops.

Any time I needed to empty my aching knackers into one,
a weak smear of tears, snot and piss, I fixed it to the wall, whispered:
I'm the rock-hard tart who's pecked his way up Thatcher's snatch!

I whipped my wet cigar out of my baby-blue trackie bottoms
quicker than it took them to smash up my tombstone.
Yours is a request that will never be played.

Vow

A black, E blank, U LAUrA, I another, O Heaven,
this last morning I'll tell of the vowels' latent spawnings;
A, black velveteen corset of flies captivates,
blusters and clusters over the cruel stench,

A pit of shit; E, spears and shields, the filigree
of glacial lace caught in my throat, an arrow-hook;
I, blood-spit and anger, laughing beauty,
I is a letter swept along the scarlet boulevard;

U, divine vibrations through viridian seas,
animal lusts flowing, alchemical sorrows
stitched into hardened arteries to derange me;

O, trumpet full of strange triumphs, blowing to bits
the silence of angels and cupids around the globe:
O, Omega, catch the violent dart of her azure eyes.

VE Day 1985

after Wayne Pratt

At the VE Night piss up, the gloom of the Blitz, the chill
Of V2s, Goering's capture, Berlin scorched, were recalled.
Then forgotten, the old girls squawking along with Al Bowlly.
On our first rendezvous we'd landed on this lot.

But this wasn't the time for cockney triumphalism;
The cheeky young man in the SS glad-rags
Tickled the dollies' flab. Pickled in gin,
They roared till they pissed their bloomers.

They fondled me and petted me and Love had to wait…
We sat up all night lost in the depths of each other's eyes,
My hand just inside your blouse. My excuse was scabies,

And you were under orders to declare your bunch of grapes.
At dawn, we walked around the railings, Clissold Park.
Inside we could hear the parakeets sounding the all clear.

Lux! and Fux!

Flesh! under Heaven's dark light the sole fruit we bite,
Sweet and sour, juicing our teeth, My Lady; my soul
Hungry solely for Love, saw you just once and, gripped
By the throat, in the mouth your tart tart choked me,

Love! the sole emotion of those who weep not
At the world's dread. Love's stones grind and mill
The arrows of the rude, the shields of the prude, into hard
Wafer, my joy this Witching Hour, my woe this Eastertide.

Love, pretty shepherd boy in a pissed peasant's dream,
Herded me into a pastoral free of animal lusts, free
Of tears, but full of vile sweet white wine, unchilled!

Flesh is the peasant dreaming feebly that triumph
Will strangle the triumphant – this Holy Day or not.
Why let ecstasy's darts fall short, Love and Flesh?

Freeview

Relief from *Comic Relief* sought, and found,
flipping past *Russia Today* onto the *ADULT Section*,
in fixing my eye upon *Babestation Academy*,
to catch you, Charity, shaking your shapely rump.

No more red plastic bulbs tweaking celebrity noses:
just your silent lips not slug-plump with botox,
your fresh breasts not yet silicone bloaters like the rest.
One small donation and I could listen to your 'filth'.

I'm tossed into the refrigerated hold of factory-line phone sex!
Unflipping catch, desire slipping through the net,
I dream of you divested of logo, mobile, and smut.

There's only one way that one way communication ends: a flick
of the switch. My weak song at your tight thong corpses,
like a weathergirl cracking a dirty joke by mistake.

You Know

It's National Poetry Day again. Duffy's
droning on the radio (again) and you're on
at the Poetry Society, whither I am headed
to undress your double offbeats with my ears.

But you've got a face like a spanked arse;
you've got a voice like a spanked arse. But
I clap along with the rest of the clowns relieved
when the prize-giving's over. You won (again)

with your thumping Great I Am in clumping iambics.
You can't beat a posy conduit for poesy's soft con job;
yet neither can you beat off love's stiff competition.

Heads you win the laurels; tails I lose Laura;
my name is reduced to a rhyme-scheme you use,
the clapped-out alternative to you-know-whose.

December 2013–March 2014

Overdubs

On the late Massacre in Piedmont (Sonnet XXI)

Avenge, O Lord, thy slaughtered saints, whose bones
Lie scattered on the Alpine mountains cold,
Even them who kept thy truth so pure of old,
When all our fathers worshipped stocks and stones;
Forget not: in thy book record their groans
Who were thy sheep and in their ancient fold
Slain by the bloody Piedmontese that rolled
Mother with infant down the rocks. Their moans
The vales redoubled to the hills, and they
To Heaven. Their martyred blood and ashes sow
O'er all th' Italian fields where still doth sway
The triple tyrant; that from these may grow
A hundredfold, who having learnt thy way
Early may fly the Babylonian woe.

John Milton

The Fugger of Wonderful Black Words

This poem is so bad I'm talking over it, so that
its feathery undersong can tickle me to laughter.
I can just catch its little breath in my throat
speaking a vapour that is odourless and democratic.
All poems are about poetry, even love sonnets in Italian.
His name is Johannes Miltoni and he loves poesy as much as you.
His lady's dark eyes flash like dancing rhymes down the page,
his metre a rumbling lower house welcoming the technocrat PM.

Berlusconi mounts his last *bunga bunga*. The girls are fresh,
winking their gussets; their crooning host is old. The poem is too,
but it heals itself like a simile that wasn't there in the original.
Did I mention that I was sitting in the toilet? I thought not.
I rise to wipe and turn to flush white noise over all of this. Don't
take me seriously. Rome burns with overdubs all the time.

(Milton: Italian Sonnets II–VI)

(for Tim Atkins)

Home Page

As tribute to save ruin to ground
repeatedly gone into the till
one hand does his fair daughter
caught with Electra's grandees in
Pandar's rotten odes of disorderly husbandry
the bawdy sways inspired spears apostrophised tasers
until he brings back booty to the sunny parade
and the things you know know nothing that knows
squeezed out of you via hooded genitals
in universal shame once
he's taken part in any panegyric
onto the pillow guides for an affidavit he
marshals dishonourable discharge but can't slash
through your rock door with his blacklist GPS.

(Milton: Sonnet VIII)

Black Edge

My shadow sweats pure light in ill-lit rooms.
I'm gathering time to see how things go – the little
customs, spells and mystifications that I'd ignored
amid wilful amnesia, eternally
recurring countdowns, temporal staggering between
glass buildings glowing with their own lucidity,
changing colour like harlots' hairdos –
all clocks removed from their façades.

My shadow will collapse into his pool of light; the place
will leave us behind without moving a muscle against us.
Labour over time and space wrestled from me, the first
knock on the door of Year Zero (rapacious
beyond responsibility) will be for him.
I will be perfectly alone with myself.

(Milton: Sonnet XIX)

Avenge

never beat the shuttered face the
stolen children tutored in Apocalypse
tortured images predictable exact
foetuses aborted while a doctor injects
small injuries with poison now
Yazidi women have been
scattered the connection breaks
the newsfeed freezes MPs
hanged from lampposts
their daughters soiled sold
but the Sun Girls now sing
they rape us so *we* kill them
scrolled down from equivalence
with Milton's slaughtery sonnet

(Milton: Sonnet XXI)

Song Net

Song net cast wide catches the drift of a lost
melody in the draft as it shades into attitude,
even contempt. Heracles carriers swing low
over your blindfold, your knuckles cut and hurting.

Cucumber off your rested eyelids, you crouch at the
keyhole, haunt the frame of honest looking:
the clientele clutches
your wrinkled flesh pages; eyes slide off the edges.

She luxuriates in her one long leg, her aching tongue
waggling tangy but loose in her blood-spit mouth.
This is not imagination but a Google search,

blind preparation for startling revelations in four
meaty stanzas. He steers this steed such as mighty
Jove might do, beyond compare, in austere deliverance.

(Milton: Sonnet XXIII)

2011–2015

Mayan Thoughts at Brighton

to the memory of Lee Harwood

A giant stone eye, stark orbital pupil, its
fringe of lashes, stares into space fixing
its four parts asserting a fifth axis, time,
which passes through this point where gulls

swoop between the knapped flint fronts
of seashore cottages muscled by glass shine.
Amid fish shop vapours greasy hands
palm second-hand books in dark interiors.

The pier is a skeletal wreck on an invisible
island: summer fights through grey in a shaft
of sunlight that lifts both steyne and twitten.

Beneath the viaduct consciousness pools;
the screen of occurrence strains expanse. But
grief? No poem will do, no poem will do it.

August 2015

New Ghost

for Lee

New red buses with their retro staircases
rush by. In the British Museum
the crowds snap with their phones every trifle
that tickles their distracted intelligence…

Far north, halfway down a new path
– new to us – we discover
the Roman bath-house, its *pilae*
holding up a phantom floor to wind and rain.

Farther down the hill, we hit the sluggish Lune,
fronted by lost warehouses
shyly turning into dwellings. Cast light

on this dimness of knowing, straining across
the expanse to take in tree or meadow or cottage.
This is a haunt of the living. Let it go.

August–September 2015

It's Nothing

Untitled

The central heating clanks into icy
silence and cool oblivion. Voices
cluttering the air waves favour
drone attacks over air-strikes, either way

to drop revenge over 'democratic deficit';
they'll only push for a vote they can win.
In earmuffs under the umbrella you can't
hear the soft rain, but believe anything

I say about the weather. By the time
it's dark, the swans turn impossibly
black, dabbling in obscure waters. In

the unheated room the light-bulb takes a full
minute to reach its intensity, by which time
I've left in cold pursuit of the future.

The Evening Star

I searched everywhere for your letter
that I know says something like *You've
got a special language for poetry,
Robert, and I haven't.* I didn't find it

but I'm trying to lose that language now as
I think of 2 freshly pulled pints of Hophead
standing on the bar in Brighton, their fog
of bubbles clearing from the bottom-up like revolution,

the clean taste of bitter pleasure,
that we could have shared, Lee. Later,
I read your last poem, emptying it out
like the mail-sack the postman in it carries,

all the messages with their special ordinary words
scattered; and I think: that's enough, that's enough.

The Duplicator

Can you make a poem out of rain?
A man pushes a pram through a haze
of drizzle. Yes you can, but what's it
singing, winking across the tarmac, gargling

in gutters? The lighthouse ignites the storm
that rushes towards dissipation; beams spark
in the gloaming. You fail to duplicate,
verisimilitude crashing the bins in gusts in

the backyard, real enough. A car put-putts
very close behind you and purrs. Not real.
Turn. You see the lights of a dream sedan
burning under the wet hump of its bonnet, the windscreen

a driverless blank wiped clean. When words
overtake you, you edge into the midst of your life.

The Lion Returns

We bail out of the Northern Line at Moorfields
and head for The Lion on the corner of Tithebarn. Dave
holds two half-pint glasses for us in readiness, slides towards
his recommendation, which we accept, with grace.

We settle with the beer, the post-work talk flipping
between love, domestic disaster, political mendacity:
the PM's bombing starting another 'war', and a Labour
leadership that leads to and fro, electoral collapse.

This fissure in obligation pauses the week, fills with joy.
We split a pork pie. The flow of the evening overtakes.
George Formby winks his 'best wishes' but we know it
can't be that simple: the station for Blackpool is a façade.

Out in the night the air chills. Good
night. The city quivers, a distant muscle.

The Crust of Miracle

Stolen by fog, sunlight returns like a spelling
to the tongue, peeping through the blue dye
sinking into viscous air, tinged orange,
until the milky film unfolds the baffled ear.

The sick duck isn't sick at all; it's a decoy
bobbing wooden among real preening fowl;
its beak droops; its curved neck sinks. Once
solved, enigma glides off-stage, empty and full.

The fallen ash tree buckled an iron fence,
its rotten fungal trunk exposed. It must have snapped
while branches wriggled as it fell, in gales,

to soften the blow, between splitting and
impact. It's easier to deride somebody's bad
spelling than to teach them to think and see.

Lyric Logic

This makes me sound like somebody else:
I've borrowed a voice for a while and parade in it,
asserting the things of the world as noisy breaths.
Could I go without saying, let every thing
speak for itself in its turn? I speak I;
I'm beside myself with words, though even this
is only one way among many. In the real world
of the classroom, I dub this 'metabiography',
whether the self is a writer reading himself into the dark,
or a reader writing her way out to the light.
Earnest and contrived, I
mean what they mean, these words;
they are thrown between us like bridges or gang-planks
and we trip across the gaps – or drop – between them.

Sonnet (Fourteen Bars)

I push to the front of my mind
problems like how to get hold of
the latest Macedonian bossa nova classic,
a brace of pheasant, and bottles of JHB,

and fill my ears with Brother Ray and Bags
grooving on stretched-limo hit singles or,
chilled, jamming through an elastic slow blues,
while I polish off the Mayne de Beauregard,

now you exit the front room, uncertain
whether you'll re-descend, leaving your pre-scribed lover,
hapless, hopeless, addicted to eternal repetition,

with this abstract lachrymose gloom
phrasing everything he feels beyond convention,
as it uncertainly pads its abject asperities across the dancing floor.

(Variation on) Ode to Life

I share a fish's unblinking view of rain on a river surface
under Lime Street station roof glass in the storm. Half
empty mid-afternoon train slips out into weather,
my mind half made up, half blowing free as though

on the platform at Edge Hill. David Bowie's dead;
yet posing by The Wall he's defiantly alive.
Floods mirror watery sun fringed by pressing cloud.
Inside: warmth, coffee. Decision making as poesis…

The train slides under the latticed crystal of Crewe
for pause. In the rhythm of yes and no, between
work and poetry, inside and outside motion and stillness

Don Pullen coaxes, knuckle-slaps, hammers his *Ode to Life*
to life; all I want is to word its wordless hopes into
this poem that will never stop

'Useless Landscape'

This song weighs the same in Tom Jobim's mouth
though its title floats free in mis-transliteration.
It takes on Wittgensteinian mass but
depresses the grace and gravity of *Without you*

it's nothing. On Church St, one of Loy's mad bums
grunts into the plastic *Intonarumori* of a toy
mic and guitar, nothing-words. Modern
boys with virginal giggles fix him

in a phone's stare, knockabout flailing:
this pitiless marionette, who could have translated
the *sotto voce* patter of wild rain for *her* brute ear…

A sharp shard in suspense meshes the patterns I find:
formal collisions hoisted. Freighted by sandbags,
ballast is sinking; the banners frap free.

(amid and between Melissa Gordon's Fallible Space,
for Sandeep Parmar)

Meaning Me

(The Belvedere)

It takes five minutes flat to work out he's a professor too.
He carries his research everywhere on a hard drive
that he pulls from his pocket – though he risks every
drug he can remember: acid, speed, dope and e. Gin.

The cosmic caveman, freshly fallen from the wagon,
shares a spoof kid's picture book called *Jack Shit*. Imagine.
The retired gigolo with one trouser leg trapped down his sock
leaps on the bar to unravel Christmas tinsel. In the back

room, Barry from the La's is playing impromptu guitar
but we don't check it out. I miss the nights when Steve used
to lean round the bar and ask, 'Fancy some Howlin' Wolf?'

This is nothing much ado about something or other, like my dream
in which a long dead neighbour from Southwick said, 'Your parents
never got something they could understand.' Meaning me.

Setting Off for Work Ahead of You

I've forgotten my reading glasses so I'm writing this
Today is one of the numbered days on the long tally
And I'm negotiating with myself about myself
I left where we left ourselves on the mattress

I might have to leave *my* European Union
The PM's negotiating hard with the Poles
Goodbye Roubaud goodbye Kouwenaar back
To a thin slice of parkin and a slim vol by Larkin

Forsythia bursts cold beside the rusty tracks warm
You're still at home negotiating your wardrobe for work
A bye-law states no one shall sing on this train

If I could read it back this might prove a love poem
Entuning our hard pleasures into our soft routine
I scratch my voice in harsh contravention of the rules

A Poem With You

Soft thighs open the spring day to sunlight,
sexual thrill in the quality of morning,
the frisson of travel: the Amphitheatre glimpsed
from the Wall, the Deva, the shell of the Civil War hall,

its sky-blue oval windows. We stand on charity,
buying clothes and CDs, catching up on popular music
45 years late. We dine at a restaurant conspicuously French
but covertly Slavic with caraway seeds thrown onto trout.

Workaday grievances rise in the holiday talk
like granite, come and go unscheduled as
women's legs under tables, seducing no one.

Reading mixed metaphors on the train home,
I'm wary of them. Part of me is still in bed,
as it should be, in such a poem, with you.

(for Patricia)

The Book of Names or: *Late at the Tate*

The bullseye breasts of the Matisse nude
follow us across the room to where his Inattentive Reader
smoulders. She's irritated and has turned from
what looks like raw pastiche of David Miller's *Visual Sonnets*.

Patricia sees the play of colour, the balance of form;
I see that frown. Later, someone calls me Richard
Patterson; he's checked on the web so that's non-negotiable.
No ogleable odalisque can help me lose this self now.

Fortuity I endorse, the strong noun Peter Riley uses
of your patient projects and restless forms.
But my dictionary gives it a wide berth. It offers

'fortuitism' instead, another ism we don't need.
We don't *believe* in chance; it happens. Then we choose.
Sonia Delaunay knocked up Tristan Tzara's pyjamas.

(to Peter Hughes at 60)

Last Look

They didn't let me swear my oath on a dictionary
not even the one containing the word 'Brexit'.
There's a lot to say but not much of it is
me. A nudge unit elbows my outcomes' income.

What can I do with competing apocalypses,
hide from the faculty bully in my office and
hum along to *How Insensitive*? We should all trespass
and trample over the bye-laws, democratic dancing.

I suspect the person I'm talking to owns a dinner jacket.
Impact is when he's rammed by a waitress
in a private dining club. *What can one do?*
The Justice Minister doesn't trust the Court of Justice.

I want to disappear this 'I' in a cloud of urb-ex dust, while
the decommissioned university crumbles over its head.

November 2015–March 2016

Breakout

didn't think

it would be like this green murk
slanted light catches the national fish basking
just below the surface black lengths wait
sluggish broody and autarkic stirring things up

for a jape the men see where
to cast their bait vote British now
it's an antonym to paki spat in
the street but the fish rest unmoved

as a terror truck ploughs into a
celebrant crowd its national day 100s of
miles away the continent we no longer
belong to our sympathy tempered by autonomy –

they've got our country back for us
and now they want it for themselves

twitter diplomatics

break shaft noises back and forth hold
hands up winking tank lit black forces
exchanging fire to drop over mid-rank chains
whose masterminded orders for those vasty super strollers

newswires unconfirm huge whichway swerving in the
headlights and clubs' high pillared floodlit facetime
in streets just glimmers on peppered iphones
chiefs on lower downs from downy drips

they are moving complete glued radio blackouts
Ataturk tanks on streets promise soldiers waving
in slanted darkness talk of confused blondes
licking microphone ice creams in slapping shame

for healing gunfire on the helicopter parliament
a secular bloodshed crowd flips every gunshot

chaos limbed

tinged by heavenly vision tingled darts folded
from ambrosia into utopian innards of gospel
bring back regrexit deserts hanging conspiracy fire
against steady English rain watch infective eye
that cannot be lidded free of cleft
bobbing head reciting poems about nothing flickable
deceit at quotidian world puzzles turned cockpits
to sticky pools of pleasure herbicidal bitterness
re-absorbed into body ink dried into pattern
a loud table of word-folds a
'French' *entrée* wilful as a *New European*
headline carnival passing girls in feathers twirling
atremble to the beat while the heat
lifts its alien rhythm to polonium cocktails

fuck the

pigmeat resting against the untended blade blandishments
of the apparatchik! speak post-truth unto powerlessness
wormholing exits within Brexit for the tweets
of the hopeful minutes and matters arriving

I've forcefed my kidnapped evil poets watercress
scrumpy and their own bad verses until
they relinquish their copyrights and I release
them tonguetied back into the wordless wild!

failure buried in a national moment infectious
as aspiration in palpable echoes of following
his workplace soviet outvotes my replete un-employability

the post-factual world lies at my feet
but I am wearing somebody else's boots
and my toes are twitching to kick!

breaking point

pointed out they all broke out of
wisdom into classic eurocratic distrexit data and
cobweb dusters thick with Londonism sneeze the
Briggering actioned by our slippy doggy do-dos

microdrone and sphericam catch the pinched elegance
cranes swing over procurement and Calais searchlights
polyglot polymaths tax a multilingual driver uncertainty
outweighs expertise they happy-houred to him

wriggling out of clown suits while offsite
unicorns gallop offshore patriots pencil conspiracy in
booths or coin puritan Corbynista temperance tempers
bumpily depicting rammed roundabouts with no exits

lorries at the border queue for inspection
(my passport to Ealing has been rescinded)

June–September 2016

Hap: Understudies of Thomas Wyatt's Petrarch

All the King's wives and all the King's Men
Couldn't put Wyatt together again

Avising the bright beams of these fair eyes
Where he is that mine oft moisteth and washeth,
The wearied mind straight from the heart departeth
For to rest in his worldly paradise
And find the sweet bitter under this guise.
What webs he hath wrought well he perceiveth
Whereby with himself on love he plaineth
That spurreth with fire and bridleth with ice.
Thus is it in such extremity brought,
In frozen thought, now and now it standeth in flame.
Twixt misery and wealth, twixt earnest and game,
But few glad, and many diverse thought
With sore repentance of his hardiness.
Of such a root cometh fruit fruitless.

Sir Thomas Wyatt

Perhaps a Mishap

Inside the poem is another poem; inside that another.
The SS guards stoop to pat the *lager* hound.
You hate the poem, its logic, its symmetries.
Somewhere, someone is giving birth on an oily rag.

They've taken a convoy of Mercedes to visit the ruins,
the diktats of a lasting piece, the master plan.
Inside the plan is another plan; you're running
through the forest with a stolen hard drive.

The dry shells of dream open as you wake – you find
no trace of relational interference. As Wyatt knows,
debugging his devices against the infant's cry,
the yearning whine of the washing machine. On

the commute from Kent he scopes the news; the fisted spider
that dissembles as a berry: one side ripening, the other rotting.

November 2016

Hap 1

Som fowles there be that have so perfaict sight

I pull down the blind on the sunny train to shield my eyes
like it's 1948 and I'm some old bird from 'the firm'
deigning to meet my dark mistress in daylight
but settling for some jazz-sweaty basement in Soho again.
I blinked at Los Alamos just in time, I'd think,
to save my sight and salve my conscience;
I signed the Official Secrets Act in black and white.

But it's 2017 and out of my reverie I'm up to town
to discuss exit strategies with the three jokers.
When Boris, swollen and unstable, asks me,
'Is there anything in this Putin-Trump-Brexit business?'
I'll say, 'Nothing,' when I'd meant to say nothing,
and I'll leap from the frying pan of my *amour-propre*
into the raging fire of his blinding ambition.

Hap 2

How oft have I, my dere and cruell foo

I hold my enemies closer than the others.
And that includes you, my dear, as we negotiate exits
from our customs union! I bow, and I scrape the floor
of your bejewelled boudoir with my silvery tongue.

This could end up with my vital organs dripping lard,
packed in attaché cases and dumped in the Thames;
or me zipped up neatly folded whole in a holdall
by an attaché from the Russian Embassy. Call that

that! I'll face this exile, banishment to Kent,
holed up alone all winter in a dead resort, a sort of spy
bleaching my back story to a blank sheet, fresh start.

I'd watch Trump's inauguration on a wobbling telly:
his thumbs, swollen with promises, up. Your pain is not my gain.
Even those back-stabbing Tories dub this 'a lose-lose scenario'.

Hap 3

Because I have the still kept fro lyes and blame

My tongue is rigid, moist in attentive silence, unlike
those of slack Brexiteers who promised the riches of the land
to a sequacious populace without delivery or deliverance.
(Wordless, it glistened down drifting down from your navel.)

Your slim leather gloves slap to the floor of the crowded train
at the feet of a young man who ignores them under his phone.
'This isn't what we wanted Feminism for,' stooping, lame;
'I just wanted the right to an abortion if I were ever raped!'

Your rights could become wrong at the flick of a tongue,
and I'd have to stand, hands behind back, tongue-tied,
beetroot-flushed at blatant bloviation, unperfected

in my studied 'Foreign Office' *sprezzatura;* minding
my mistress in Camberwell with her proofs of the next Mantel,
my wife and kids with the washing machine back in Kent.

Hap 4

Ever myn hap is slack and slo in commyng

Whatever happens happens. Slack comings or
stern desire. I'll take it or leave it. She loves me
not. These paper jousts of the pastime tiger
make brittle kindling for a heartless fire.

So snow shall rest unmelting on her black hair;
the Atlantic shall drain to leave a Grand Canyon
for our special relationship; the crowded Thameslink south
shall be free of their spy crouched behind *The Sun*;

before I shake off this sweat of conspiracy, this
fear of wrongful arrest (and the rest). I'm as bitter and twisted
as Kentish beer – culpable sweetness covers her winy secrets,

saccharine wasteland where I build my shanty trust,
a refugee camp that I can no longer police – now I arrive.
I'm wired, wired-up, Wyatt. Anything could happen.

Hap 5

Was I never yet of your love greved

A dead file with your name on it (and mine)
could finish me off, just as I'm commissioned
to speak in *propria persona*. No longer aping
Petrarch or Plutarch for the first first lady,

I'm filing a report to frame the second's dark portrait.
I'm impelled to dredge the linings of Eurocrats' stomachs,
with a posting to Brussels in the last days should I fail.
On the last night the umbrella tip might sting my vitals.

Don't touch me! I shall persist, though you insist on tears
(mine). You're right on rights, the environment, nukes, yet
you're squawking like one of Trump's tweets in CAPS!

Cause and effect is affected by metatruths and his dispatches
but you'll only bring the flat (or the axe) down on your head:
you're the last cause of everything I hold dear, LOSER!

Hap 6

Caesar, when that the traytor of Egipt

Theresa, when grasped by the tiny hand of the tyrant,
presented on a plate the guts of the NHS, and smiled,
as his long red tie tickled his glans, though she sweated
beneath a grand's worth of leather trousers, unaroused.

I jetted trans-Alpine to our 'European allies' with friable promise.
If only I could rope Remoaner Reginald Pole to the pole,
slop inflammable beard balm over his hipster bush, my eyes
watering at the garlicky aroma of barbequed traitor, and

disgorge my stomach as he blisters! Duplicitous spider am I:
her fake furs and my fake news brushed smooth and receptive
to time and season, de-briefing, and briefing, on fake leather couches.

No other way to say this, so I don't: We must quit loving!
She grabs me by the man-pussy and I roll over into deceit's
thick web: I'll tell anything, promise everything.

Hap 7

Love and fortune and my mynde, remembre

I'm taking the rap (again) between these sheets (alone)
or undercover in Brussels. My mind presents present promise
against the presence of the past, which is expiring faster than
my EU passport. (When I speak like that I wish I were dead.)

I'm out of sorts (with love, with you), and the *failing* pound
leaves me out of pocket here after one sour greuze and,
out of my mind, I crank myself up in the middle of the night,
to rub out my heretic Reginald like a furious youth!

Pleasure is a gif file on repeat: your breasts swinging.
All I'll bring back from Europe will be re-memories of England.
I'll be through these hapless sonnets before we hit the worst.

My fortunate face peppers with glass, my untrue heart splintered:
iron discipline shatters the one-way mirror during illicit interrogation,
its evidence as inadmissible as happiness.

Hap 8

I find no peace and all my war is done

'I am a difficult poet in Kent' (Charles Bernstein)

I jet above the world's woolly defence. My hubris clouds over.
I've been withdrawn from Brussels. Draw no conclusions from
                                                           [*The Daily Hate.*
I've nothing in my diplomatic bag, yet all of Europe fructifies beneath;
I fear I'll be frozen out from Boris, dried out in Frinton again.

Love of my country (and *her*) loosened my tongue, but now
I'm as tight as a berry. I'm unsafe in this safe house,
dark space for my dark place, like Pole's mum on the block
when her head went *splat! splat! splat!* ha-ha.

I'm fixed in Brexitland permafrost, purr warm words about soft power.
I'm the Baptist of a British Anthropocene, the Commonwealth of
                                                               [Big Data.
I love it all, yet my wife alone loves the washing machine man, a Pole.

I pull the wrong face in the wrong sonnet and it weeps ha-ha.
This unreformed pleasure is the cause of *my* back-pocket
schadenfreude: Paul Nuttall's fake degree from Edge Hill.

Hap 9

Who so list to hounte I knowe where is an hynde

Once I chased you round your flat, dear heart,
and we fucked like rabbits until we were sore; or,
spread on your Field of the Cloth of Gold bedspread, you spread;
or rose, wild, to be mounted, and I came from behind.

I thought of that moment before (in Brussels): when
your loose gown fell from your shoulders, but you slipped
naked through my toils to your toilet, fishnets void.
I served up this reverie of service to myself.

You other me into the last lover on your long list;
I spy through your bedroom keyhole: you service yourself
with your G-spot rabbit, and your felt-tip banner from

the Anti-Trump March teases: *KEEP YOUR HANDS OFF
MY REPRODUCTIVE RIGHTS!* You are your own lover first.
'This *last* time,' you say, 'I'll tie you up and toss you off!'

Hap 10

The longe love, that in my thought doeth harbar

Length is measured by my wife's receptivity.
She holds *him* close with his in-your-face toolbox,
his bulging bag of bolts, his lengthy wrench.
His white van parks in her drive. She spreads

ambassadorial safe conduct for this envoy of joy!
Trust him to pull himself, and lust's negligee, off.
His hard thrust celebrates the National Insurance U-
turn. He takes *her*, but who takes the photograph?

Back early, I find them arranged as on the *Punting
in Kent* Twitterfeed that Gove had notified me of:
gaping bacon pulsed upon her washing machine top.

I'll sliver his liver! Across the shire he speeds in his
fishnet codpiece, hiding in oasthouses and dogging sites.
But first, I'll slash his tyres and send for the crusher.

Hap 11

Suche vayn thought as wonted to myslede me

Lost in the deserted estates of East Kent, I live
alone with my vanity project – translations of lost
sonnets – absented from PM, and wife, and mistress:
disgraced by the first; the wife cast out in shame;

the clean break with my mistress's dirty love (but the loss
of her dodgy intel). She won't pick up: I cast myself down
on the couch. On TV I watch the terror attack
at Westminster, lockdown of the palace of liberty,

from where May promised to mend our broken shires
but stumbles now over a homily to human rights. Amid
the broken bodies all I see is *her* lost face, like thunder,
electric lightning sex, compressed code – cold comfort

as they come for me, at last. Recalled from unquiet
solitude, emboldened by accusation, I cry, *Bring it on!*

Hap 12

Me thynkethe my head is with childe, alas!

I frame my defence in the dark tower
but my words disappear as they are written.
The sticky fog of accusation licks at my heels
and I stumble, lashing out at my shadow.

Headache fills this cell: heartache fuels the world.
Unsheath my poison pen. My rapier wit slashes
against these slash-stained walls. This sonnet is as fake
as the witness is false – *and* as the dream I lose you in.

I awake in a modern office, wire chairs in an oval:
the complainant's script flaps like a tongue on his lap.
My stab at the State Bard proves inadmissible and

I'm freed. But the next time the boss says to me
All my wives looked like Honeysuckle Weeks,
I'll just smile, enigma's secret groom.

Hap 13

Auysing the bright bemes of these fayer Iyes

Look at the glowering greed in their eyes.
Many (almost most) weep to hear the Trigger triggered
while talk of 'Henry VIII powers' taxes the dirty mind
in a Kentish paradise of 'villages and hamlets' where
guys in slacks sip bitter and compare the legs
of Mrs May and Nicola Sturgeon.

Between misery and wealth, principle and ambition,
few are glad, and the Many have no Plan B (or A): but
soft Regrexit for Hard Brexit as repealers unspin.

Espy through Edenic cobwebs of gardening leave
spun across the complaints and appeals procedures,
those frost cravings delivered to Bruxelles on spurs of fire.

Brought to such extremes thought freezes
though its bearer stoops unthinking into flame.

Hap 14

Yf amours faith, an hert vnfayned

If honesty bubbles on the hob unboiled
If mad policy tempered by my diplomatic tweaks
breeds festering slough thwarted desire
If you think less of the electorate than of the elect
If the Brexiteer's battle-bus with its cashback payback
U-turns on a blind corner (as IDS pleads to camera!)
If every thought (Quiet Wyatt!) cartoons on my brow
as my croaky voice now gruff now falsetto (and false!)
blurts or tweets the alt. facts bare-faced for you
If Boris's 'piccaninny' show is hardly worth blacking up for
If wailing sirens on Westminster Bridge burn sorrow into anger
If feverishness for athletic tricks freezes out my old mistress
If I am destroyed by love riding hard
the fault is mine the irredeemable convenience yours

Hap 15

My galy charged with forgetfulness

My Harley Low Rider charges without a doubt
across the potholed tarmac of Austerity;
steering between my rock and their hard place,
I roar helmeted, Boris still forgetful of my loyalty.

Every piston of this mid-life-crisis indulgence
fires me on towards my death. Torqued to the asphalt,
I fart my way over bumpy hillocks, a boil on my butt.
(But who took the photo? Who 'suggested' *he* 'send for' me?)

Blanket cloud, sheet rain, on the M20. The spray from
Euro-lorries tests my skidding, and I swerve, and yet
still I serve, despite my confessed 'error', their half-truths.

I no longer read the starry messages I courier across Christendom
and Kent. Drenched in shame beyond reason: I stand,
deliver the 'goods', then tear up the back roads to Nowhereland.

January–April 2017

Hap Hazard

This poem is the un-perished part of another,
and behind that, the other poem, the one in foreign,
as behind Theresa May there squats the succubus
of Thatcher, donning the rubber masks of Englishness.

From east to west Wyatt charges on his Harley;
from brunette to blonde he changes his like to true Anglo,
thundering sparkplugs and sparkling blue eyes.
Wobbling, he'll only live for six more English lines.

His pen admonishes the knaves of Kent, caught dallying
with 'lactating maids' at Maidstone. In plaintive woe,
he issues this feverish prophecy of his unquiet mind:

'They're all struck dumb by May's lightning election call:
Corbyn at stool, Boris mid-bullying, his Bullingdon bull,
all her enemies routed in one swift English retreat.'

(for Robert Hampson)

April 2017

Surrey with the Fringe on Top

By the waie as hee went, hee heerd of another Earle of Surry besides himselfe, which caused him make more hast to fetch me in, whom hee little dreamed off had such arte in my budget, to separate the shadow from the bodie.
—Thomas Nashe

Th'Assyrian king, in peace, with foul desire
And filthy lusts that stain'd his regal heart;
In war, that should set princely hearts on fire,
Did yield vanquisht for want of martial art.
The dint of swords from kisses seemed strange;
And harder than his lady's side, his targe:
From glutton feasts to soldier's fare, a change;
His helmet, far above a garland's charge:
Who scarce the name of manhood did retain,
Drenched in sloth and womanish delight.
Feeble of spirit, impatient of pain,
When he had lost his honour, and his right,
(Proud time of wealth, in storms appalled with dread,)
Murder'd himself, to shew some manful deed.

Henry Howard, Earl of Surrey

The Unfortunate Fellow Traveller

The Soote Season

As in a shit encore to *The Sound of Music*, with which
the hills are reportedly alive, although eary valleys
are plugged with cotton-wool mist in denial of the results,
the actors have returned, re-shuffled as themselves.

A young pigeon ruffles its feathers but an old gull plummets,
far from disputed shores, to stab with blooded beak
the fledgling, flapping broken-winged to its death, on
Birmingham New Street platform 5. The national fish loafs.

The snakeskin shoes of Theresa May kick off –
as *she* does, rolled into the padded cell with the DUP
crying *Brexit means Brexit means Brexit…* Go re-apparitions
at Rural Affairs, to monitor moistly our dogging sites.

I dreamt *I* was in Kent; the bus missed my stop in the dark. You
don't have to be Gummer to guess this summer will be a bummer!

Set Me Free

Turn the heat up on EU negotiations
Or switch the air con to full and freeze my misty words mid-air
Let me step outside round the back where there aren't any reporters
Or Britain First heavies badmouthing Ramadan first aiders

Stick me at the bottom of the pile or send me over the top
Trap me in the smoking dark or shed some light on flammable cladding
Under clear skies of electoral peace or in the fog of class war
With a crowd of eco-crusties or a bunch of Corbyn kids

Set me up to fail on ground floor in penthouse or basement
Or halfway up where fire spreads like a whisper
Tie me down or set me free wherever I am
Up Heptonstall in gales or crashing below Hebden's floodline

Or choked in Grenfell Tower or jogging along the canal path
You're my only half hope in a world turned contrarious

His purpose lost: Her smiling grace

George Osborne isn't the god of love anymore.
It's Bo and when he's not sitting on his hands
he's sitting on my face so I can't hear his latest gaffe.
I'm as horny as fuck and I want to knock one out.

Cladding is combustible, my lady confirms. Baubles round
her neck above a slice of bust clack and cluck fake humanity.
Her love is as tough as a courtesy coffee with an EU goon
droning building regs 'red tape'. We're fuming. And hurting. And dying.

Coward Bo has buggered off. He can't remember a thing
in the Queen's Speech. That's one filthy job but royals do it
'for the greater good of the people' we're told (by them). He's
lurking, a wanker in the woods waiting to have his balls sucked dry.

Wyatt versioned this one and did it better. But at least *my* plumber
ploughs his alliterative plunger through the Thetford thicket.

(for Sean Bonney)

Chilling Venom

Zoom in on hot divided Cyprus (where Patricia was born.
She'll not get an EU passport out of that cold fact!):
Archbishop Makarios and his arch-enemies still cohabit,
melting stony hearts and green lines to ice and ire.

Frozen fire rages in a metaphor that's not Petrarch's this time;
every boiling passion evaporates self in chilly sonnets.
Sweat it out. It raves. It expires. Like freedom snuffed quick
into long despair, it's nothing; you're nothing!

Actually, I'm quite something on the dogging circuit,
out in anonymous snow, nipples erect, skin marbled,
as Bo and Go, stalking with bubbling venom, meet at my bumper –
and freeze! Limp, they pop it away and limp away, singing:

This smock's no camouflage out here in the woods
where bears shit with soulful moan and easeful sighs.

Lay Apart Your Cornet Black

They'll never recognise you, babe, if you wear that black hat,
in heat or chill, to shield your pancake from the snapping,
the clicking, the flicking and the Tweeting, while you bend
to slurp like a fancy chimpanzee with a banana.

I'd fancy a bit of Norfolk rough like you up Gas Hill,
to adorn my fatal escutcheons for *Hello* magazine.
Loafing against Wyatt's broken pillar, scratching my codpiece,
I keep my self to myself, while you spread yours across the Heath.

Your golden hair is clad in black. Your smile bleeds badly
from your facelift (as Trump would Tweet – and he should know).
Wyatt said I was 'Museless', but I thought he said 'useless':
I'm consumed in my craving, withdrawn after withdrawal, dosed
                                                                                 [by a dose.

Amid the summer sweat, or in the steaming frost of winter,
I've lost my self sorely, the Playboy of the Eastern Counties.

The Waves Work Less and Less

Nothing moves. Everything silent. The pale moon glows
behind the curtain like a Japanese dancer. Hurry Surrey!
The sea is calm tonight. The Dutch coast gleams.
The great roar of pebbles sucks your joy off, flings your woes.

Archaic fishery conventions or priapic inconvenience
drown you, drowsy in woozy pleasure, stinging pain,
in the small print of Go's encyclical, or playing with Bo
nocturnal beach volley ball with bare-breasted nymphs…

Wake up! Your dream within my dream is fled.
I impose direct rule from my writing desk.
(That would have made a neat last couplet
but it came too soon, as you too, my lord, did.)

Awake, you shout down your overspend on tapestries.
Beware where acknowledged legislators clash by day.

Lively Dooms Gather at the Last

Clips of Mistress Arundel's golden showers fast find her
fast new friends, and feed fake news-feeds with bad form.
They'll call in dodgy favours from Bo and Go whose windows
you've skilfully (but stupidly) my lord, broken with stones!

They've seen the lot and gather round in Thetford Forest
to cast their seed, with others, upon her perfect beauties. Sorry
Surrey: she has gone and you're a goner. Rear your head,
your coat of arms: both shall be chopped lordlessly from thee!

So! That's settled. Suxit! No U-turns on this one.
They can have his priory lands in Thorpe; *I* elect to snatch
his poems, both the knocked off Euroverse and his Britpo ones,
to deface them then with fancies new, mine all mine!

But no, I'm nothing but a whisper in a rustling thicket.
I blur in the background, like Bo at his last EU photo-shoot.

Direct Rule

Direct Rule: Windsor Walls

Like a man filming his wife taking a selfie
of her silvered face in sylvan Windsor Park, this poem
is a record of its own discovering. Lusty? Very!
'This is such a pleasant spot to stain with pleasure:

the picnic tables, the rustic spread, the chorus of wasps
around the bin,' the Rake from Hell remarks, pulling
his vest back on but feeling well pissed off, though
sporting in my similes. He shelters like a spent penny.

Do I have a duty of care for him, as when I share the mouldy
minibus with our student interns? No: he can sigh smoke
in my face and bugger off with his self-regarding floozy.

It's just his smoke that causes this lachrymatory response:
my voice trapped in a poem can only cry in words. They say
talking about suicide doesn't make students top themselves. It does.

Direct Rule: Ghostly Geraldine and Others

I know two women called Geraldine, both fun
to party with; both write poetry. Surrey's Geraldine
grew up in Ireland like Patricia (but she'll not get
a passport with that fact either). Lord Strange of

Knockin is knocking on his prison wall, racist twaddle
about growing up in white Britain with pure princes.
Surrey was like that, cursing new men and mere women.
You can see it in the way he traces the pedigree of Geraldine.

He found her at Hampton Court but lost her in Windsor.
Petrarchan petting! At the end of the poem he gives her away
like an evil relative at a shot-gun wedding. I wish he'd done
something with this poem. I wish I'd done something

with my life, like jousting at a tourney, or wearing the bays
as I overdub every bad poem for my lady with worse.

Direct Rule: What Virtues Rare

Praise the diversity of diversities Fox and Dox will fund
(Post-Brexit) but don't divulge their private incomes
Blow talk of generous public sector pay (and pensions)
Across the lively head of a half pint of English mild

There are no students in this poem yet their standing debt
Has nurtured a collective electorate that forms beyond
The 'envies' of petit bourgeois consumerism
This semantic field is manured with usurers' tears

Leave Surrey's hero alone (whom he dares not name) beyond ambition
The vampires settled like leeches on his fiery arms
He was far ahead of his time because he was escaping the past
But now it's one of those days in sovereign global Britain

Either moderate as a diplomat the blue plaque treatment
Or kiss the ground like a drunken student alighting at Lime Street

Direct Rule: Huge Power and Sinful Sleep

Like a policeman on leave in Liverpool, this poem can't shake
off its look: it's partly another poem (the one on which
I rest my writing pad so I can't read it anymore): the poem
with Alexander the Great no less. It alludes to Wyatt's *Psalms*.

But I'm pointing (look!) to Wyatt's *Penitential Sonnets*,
the ones I did, relating Wyatt's concupiscence and peccability.
The students gravely grind these poems into notes, while Wyatt *dies*
in his mistress's arms again, punning away like a Tudorbethan jokebook.

Even putting it on Twitter won't get Bo and Go or Fox and Dox
to RT it or DM me. Trump's bitter fruit hangs like fake outsider art
on the wailing wall of his mirrored pout. Some of these bastards
are going to need a footnote (if we're lucky) like Darius and Uriah.

They weren't lucky. Click *here* to access Sheppard's 'aesthetic justice'.
Then act it out all over the show like it's a metaphor for real justice.

(for Charles Bernstein)

Direct Rule: In Peace with Foul Desire

In peacetime, no warriors in frillies will defy this decree:
'These "suicidal fairies" can't be trusted to blow things up
and kill people with overwhelming force,' his spokesman said.
Gender's stiff agenda. But Trump's all trump and no guano!

Surrey's Saradanapalus is clearly a 'sissy', the sort to say,
I *love* balloons but nobody knows what makes 'em fly!
As our man says: What's the point of nuclear weapons
if you can't use 'em? Kim Jong-un knows how to make them fly.

O Filthy lust! Your Russian drenched the couch Obama touched.
Inhuman masculinity is 'unmanly' in my book. Books! Who
reads poetry anymore, let alone a trans translation?

Feeble and febrile, if he ever faces dishonour, loses his right to govern,
I fear that, out of his wealth in a storm of rage, he'll rise,
thumb on button, and whoosh us all to show some 'manful' deed.

31st July 2017: Passchendaele Centenary

Direct Rule: Enemy to My Knees

I guide this warrior-poet from a renaissant land, who says:
They call me the Beast of Boulogne. The enemy was well
dagged with arrows; Fox and Dox brake their staves and maces
upon the blooded Frenchmen's cracking Euro-bones!

But what of your flat-footed, crooked-ankled, squint-eyed, men?
Oh them! he said. Or your debts? Oh! those, he said. Your dad
would bury you alive to survive! (He will!) My only enemy – this
is the poem speaking – lies within! (Not so, chortle Bo and Go.)

If battered Boulogne is rendered then Daddy would push for Calais:
you'd be in charge of its refugee camp, its post-Brexit duty-free,
the English border! But you are in servitude to your fantasy:
your self, its pleasing pain, that coat of arms, this portrait.

You're going to bugger it up, mounted on your clanking nag,
easing toward that ill-at-ease, easy answer.

Direct Rule: While Life did Last that League was Tender

Mary Shelton in Wyatt's acrostic tripped down the margins
of a masterly pastime, played by Master Clere in her plackets.
He was your dogging dog, my lord, on hand with his hand.
His victories of Boleyn and Boulogne conflate in your bad spelling.

Was it a wheeze to watch Kelso flaming, huddled close as
twenty villages and hamlets and crops were scorched?
At Landrecy you were saluted by enemy fire, reprimanded by Bo.
At Montreuil, with four hundred starved French before,

and six hundred slaughtered after, you left a thousand
glorious English corpses curated for your Brexit show.
You ordered the captains forward. *Clere* saved your life…

Remember when you were both students at Cambridge?
You booted that beggar, burnt a £20 note in front of his hooter.
You're having a last laugh alone, in your last, lost, sonnet.

June – August 2017

Elegaic Sonnets

from Charlotte Smith

Petrarch of Petworth: the Earl of Sussex

Sonnet XIV: From Petrarch

Loose to the wind her golden tresses stream'd,
Forming bright waves, with amorous Zephyr's sighs;
And tho' averted now, her charming eyes
Then with warm love, and melting pity beam'd.
Was I deceiv'd?—Ah! surely, nymph divine!
That fine suffusion on thy cheek, was love;
What wonder then those beauteous tints should move,
Should fire this heart, this tender heart of mine!
Thy soft melodious voice, thy air, thy shape,
Were of a goddess—not a mortal maid;
Yet tho' thy charms, thy heav'nly charms should fade,
My heart, my tender heart could not escape;
Nor cure for me in time or change be found:
The shaft extracted, does not cure the wound!

Charlotte Smith

Where the green leaves exclude the summer beam

Brambles stick to my shirt, rip my forearms;
I tramp into the gloomiest thicket, which clings
to this gentle slope of England. The river, low,
sluggish, opens its muddy palms in resignation.

I am my thoughts, and others' thoughts, that
think through me, and she appears through me,
as I, translated, through another, transgendered, so,
like sonnets torn to shreds by cut-throat tradition.

She's a voice clawing in my throat: 'Unhappy Pet,
you're wasting your prime, as limp as my glove
that you've secreted to sniff amid the confetti porn.[1]

I'm beyond such thorny hope or horny desperation:
but even if I were still alive, panting in Avignon,
those Brexit devils I fear would deny me a visa to visit.'

---

[1] 'Those who, like myself, frequented the Downland copses of the 1970s, will remember, with querulous humour, the prevalence of shredded pages of soft pornographic magazines amongst the undergrowth. It seems that, like the turfcutter and the charcoal burner, the rural masturbator is a type long vanished from our landscape, though he arouses little of the nostalgia and regret of the other cases.' (Earl of Sussex)

Ye vales and woods! fair scenes of happier hours

Uplands and Downlands, those scenes of Cowboys
and Indians enacted behind fishbox barricades
in Father's waistcoat and Mother's high heels,
and gulls' feathers, and beads, you bore and saw them all:

my first stirrings amid the furze, the stolen kiss
by the stile, you sniffing my stiffie like a dog: but
now you're Dead! Or Alive! beyond the high horizon,
bitter, withered, incontinent on the Continent!

Do you remember that 78, Julie London's *Cry Me a River*
echoing into crackly silence, like memory erasing its trace
of remembrance, empty as the urn that shall spill your ashes
upon the dark earth of a tannoid Tuscan vineyard,
to fructify the richest vintage that, in the 1970s,
we'd have sniffed once and poured down the sink?

Loose to the wind her golden tresses streamed

Loose blonde hair flickering in purple discotheque lights
or starchy with spray in the back of a cream Zephyr?
False lashes lashing lies through mascara tears or
laughing in Laura Ashley smocks to Van's *Warm Love?*

Did I deceive myself, tar caking my knees,
that your squint out to sea was the look of love,
that your beauteous tints should move, move me forever,
like Sonja Kristina reciting Eliot?[2] Haughty,

you warbled *Kum ba yah* in assembly, heaved
padded breasts in the pervy English teacher's *Bacchae*.
They tell me you now look just like your mother did,
so my double vision is double occasion for this *double entendre*.

A weepy meat injection extracted at Preston Park
will never furnish a cure under Brighton Pier.

---

[2] Listen to 'Piece of Mind' on Curved Air's *Air Conditioning* for the recitation from *The Waste Land*.

Oh! place me where the burning noon

Set me down on the Downs where Brexit beacons blaze
Or set me up to freeze in my blazer teasing the crumbling cliff-edge
Let me look as sexy as Corbyn cracking through the crisis of Capital[3]
Or as frigid as May defending the bankers and Bonkers Boris;
'The temple bells they say... er... come you back you English soldier...'
'You're on mic. Not a good idea.' 'What?' '*Not* appropriate!'[4]

Get me 61 winters' worth of homegrown turf and bed memories
To carpet this sonnet with springy rhythm and spongy love
I bet Surrey did this better getting head on Beachy Head
Let me cure you both of your everlasting lamentables with a
Sussex joke: 'Do people jump off here often?' 'No! Only once!'

Whoops! *That really was an elegy for himself* cried Charlotte
It's the way he would have wanted to have gone laughed Laura
Down

---

[3] See the speech Corbyn delivered at the Labour Party Conference 2017 in Brighton.

[4] Johnson misquotes the Sussex poet Kipling's verses about Burma, as Charlotte Smith, in these four poems, is ventriloquising Petrarch. Kipling's 'colonial-era poem' (to quote the media) was judged inept for spontaneous recitation during Johnson's official trip as Foreign Secretary to Myanmar (before the genocide of the Rohingya, it is worth recording, as is the genocide).

The South Downs Way

Sonnet XLIV: Written in the church-yard at Middleton in Sussex

Press'd by the Moon, mute arbitress of tides,
While the loud equinox its pow'r combines,
The sea no more its swelling surge confines,
But o'er the shrinking land sublimely rides.
The wild blasts, rising from the western cave,
Drives the huge billows from their heaving bed;
Tears from their grassy tombs the village dead,
And breaks the silent sabbath of the grave!
With shells and seaweed mingled, on the shore,
Lo! their bones whiten in the frequent wave;
But vain to them the winds and waters rave;
They hear the warring elements no more:
While I am doom'd—by life's long storm opprest,
To gaze with envy, on their gloomy rest.

Charlotte Smith

To the South Downs

Ah! there you are again, O! beloved slopes
with your wind-combed Ring of huddled beeches,
rising from narrow paths whose nettles sting and
dock leaves soothe, where I belted it out like *Bessie* Smith.

O! beloved slopes, your clump remains, now
unapproachable, glowing like a Paul Nash design
in a glazed false memory the poem has fired for me.
I no longer shout the blues; they just trans transport me.

O! Adur, by Bramber you flowed, where midges bit one year,
and plagues of ladybirds choked life from the stem;
the dragonfly's rainbow sank in willow bank drizzle.

Ah! no! – all nature is in drag; and so am I.
Knowing's washed away by paint or rain, but
never by trickle-hush tears. The blue remains.

To the River Adur

Along the river-track, the concrete dug-outs
and flinty Saxon churches tell a walker's pulse,
while light planes glide to bump the field
and circuit the flats again, full-throttle. Ghosts

of poems haunt the refluent Adur. Lee Harwood
pausing on this bank to lift his ear to catch the skylark's
witter against the engine drone. By dusk, in his notebook,
the long shadow of a beech stops well short of allegory –

as I step into somebody else's 'romantic setting':
mantled rocks fringe a classic stream of unlikely wild waves,
the meadow a blanket of Sorrow rather than misty-wet clover.

A grisly event took place in Lewes. Bearded men dishing out
self-satisfied shoddy. Robert, promise never to organise
a 1960s conference! Must off to plunge in the briney, Lee

To the Naiad of the Adur

Come, suburban Naiad! seek a naiant channel
to the Hermaphrodites' Cave, as actual
as the 'funny men' Mother warned me of when I rambled
to and fro, in autumn or spring, on the luxuriant Downs.

I sport with these sinuous she-males in their pool,
breasts brushing the swell (and me) until a dirty old man
dishabilitates in gorse and they leap up erect, surprise attack,
to tackle his perversity with their polyamorous tackle:

bum him until his prostate liquefies like a rotting peach
with a split pip!
                Where was I? Up the Adur with such ardour,
where there's neither cave nor pool? Drown me in your

Lethean waters where I'll remember neither one thing
nor the other, beyond tidal dialectics, dispersed
in a thousand unsexed voices of two dozen Sussex poets.

Composed during a walk on the Downs

Low clouds, merging into mist that clothes
the slopes, blanket the sky and these chalk-tipped brims.
There aren't many vultures on the Downs,
the odd wallaby, renegade parakeets, a furtive puma.

Nothing under leaf-mould flowerbeds, twiggy and hard, stirs.
Swathed in duffle, I'm an inventory of invented memories,
flowing with chalky milk that swells Kingston Lane gutters
on a wet walk home, drained downhill, dammed with twigs.

By the shore, a hopeful Mermaid flips her luscious tail
outside the Pilot where, Father warns, 'Queers,
Hags and Sailors' huddle in an Edward Burra interior,

while, in the car park, the carefree Vulture munches its way
through the furred kidneys of a chalkland swain, staked
through the heart for voting Remain and for sodomy.

Written in the church-yard at Middleton in Sussex

St Nick's was washed away about thirty years
after my death, half a century since I'd perched on its flint wall
in the October moonlight, my feet in the swell,
my face salty with spray, tapping on my Psion –

as soon as they append your town's name with 'on-sea'
you're in trouble; sea levels and longshore drift crumble
the clear edges of England, like French marauders up the Adur
imposing EU Directives by the ghost-bridge at Botolphs –

tapping about bodies tipping out of floating coffins
into the brine, gloomy-Halloweeny-style, wreathed
in weeds, and rising on the bleaching tide to admonish me:
Cheer up Charlie-Girl, you're only dead once!

No. You've escaped the names on your tumbling tombs;
I'm dead over and over, washed over, but never wished away.

On leaving a part of Sussex

You're Petrarch and Laura rolled into one
cornball of misery on Southwick Hill, but
you're not anti-binary; you're anti-everything;
not becoming woman but unbecoming woman

with a brain full of bullshit and cowpat!
You stuck out a mile in the Ladyboys of Bognor,
bigging yourself up in Bignor like you owned the place.
You'd be walking the South Downs Way, believe me,

after wild frenzy with Tom of Findon –
or with a femdom Alpha bitch in Fulking Dungeon,
nettle-thrashing you, Unworthy of Worthing! No!

I'm Madam Hamlet of Hambrook, mooching down the Avenue
at dusk, listening out for hedgehogs rustling
and nightingales hammering out the blues in the mulch.

To the Insect of the Gossamer; or:
I Heard It Through the Grapevine

This is Sun Radio broadcasting from Truleigh Hill
The ether threaded with our Sunday jokes and jingles
And woven with back to back singles like *Bad Moon Rising*
(Father's atom-bomb radar bunkers beneath this furze)

My little voice is lost in this form like a poet's
While I spin the banned *Je t'aime* till it's fucked
But when the swift wireless telegraphy Nazis raid
You shout that our free radio beam escapes their cloud

Shoots beyond the stars and that visionary youth
Shall breathe a rainbow bridge of dope smoke over
The Shoreham-by-pass as we're snapped off into aerial static

Monday's dull realities rock in and roll off
Like the traffic you track for the Port Authority 9–5
We're just two little boys with our radio toys

The sea view

Big Bo-Peep is having his kip, his flock nibbling
the soft turf where my emigrants once panted
towards the French coast squeezed between sea and sky,
now locked in detention centres, milking the NHS.

He dreams of a pastoral past when 'trannie' meant a radio
for Father to listen to the Test Match on these cliffs;
and of future free trade with ... *No-New-Zea-land-Lamb!*
bleats a dream-ram, as a colonial cowboy milks himself

and melts away – no sheep-dogging delight tonight!
He's jolted awake to matching dark patches, in sky, and on sea.
Are they grey EU gunboats firing on our freighters,
our entrepreneurs smuggling flammable cladding,

the dead and the dying dumped in the English Channel
as France dowses England's chalk redoubt in cheap cheese? No.

Written in a tempestuous night,
on the coast of Sussex, December 1791

She dreamt about what the dream had called
'distributive orgasm', a rash of pleasure
that thrashes across the shingle in a wave
and roars out into the night like thunder.
Lightning streaks of delight tingle in flashes that snap
shot chalk and turf crashing to the shore, giddy
with passion. Like cognition, ecstasy is embodied
in every thing that bends to the south-west wind and yet waves on.
Led by a wan moon, her groaning body feels its passage
as she plods, soaked to the skin, shivery, shrinking
from her drawing room encounter with a horny bluestocking.
'I'm straight!' she'd protested. 'So's spaghetti until
it's wet!' the devilish dike had laughed, diving. In the whole
of quivering creation, she has no idea what spaghetti is.

Not Written at Bignor Park in Sussex, in August 1799

Mutterings from Brexit creeps and sappy racists
mingle with rhubarb squeaking, as mist steams off
the ridge of the Downs, and I hear that another
handy minister has groped his way to the exit –

Not Bo, no; as he 'understands it', he
can say Nazanin was 'training journalists in Persia'
and convince us all that *he's* been misunderstood.
He'd trade Hezbollah for his bollocks.

It'll pass! like backhanders to Israeli generals,
leaving me on this rabbit-softened turf at last
where cold war radar stations are buried intact,
like a lunch break sex toy in a strangled Tory.

The sun burns the mist off in seconds.
Its scorched earth sweep crackles through the air.

September–November 2017

Non-Disclosure Agreement

"We're very slowly edging towards a position which is very close to where we are already."

—BBC correspondent on Brexit negotiations

Sonnets from the Portuguese 38

First time he kissed me, he but only kissed
The fingers of this hand wherewith I write,
And ever since it grew more clean and white,...
Slow to world-greetings... quick with its 'Oh, list,'
When the angels speak. A ring of amethyst
I could not wear here plainer to my sight,
Than that first kiss. The second passed in height
The first, and sought the forehead, and half missed,
Half falling on the hair. O beyond meed!
That was the chrism of love, which love's own crown,
With sanctifying sweetness, did precede.
The third, upon my lips, was folded down
In perfect, purple state! since when, indeed,
I have been proud and said, 'My Love, my own.'

Elizabeth Barrett Browning

Brazilian Sonnets

> A flower, of course!
> She neither sews nor spins – and takes no thought
> Of her garments … falling off.
> —Elizabeth Barrett Browning

Thou hast thy calling to some palace-floor

Rush off, behind shades, tinted windscreens,
honing the rhymes of your prize-dick limerick.
Behind your hunch, palace functionaries hand-toss
at rumours of my fecundity, and wink.

This stage is too poor for your puffy part: daily,
you needs must announce a cross-channel bridge
or a new shining complex manured on dark bodies.
Here behind the latch let me count your gold.

The roof of our love-nest hosts noisome finches;
it's infested with mice scratching at your cricket bat.
On Sky News you applaud the Shithole President.

You think you are the thinking woman's idiot
with your phallocratic notches. A voice within chants:
It's me, calling you back, alone, the Wimpole resident.

And wilt thou have me fashion into speech

Flicked on the President's Club skirt and bustier –
without a word, bore a candle to your Euro-sceptic table.
Big Tease, a blonde wave of black-tie lust huffing
genital generosity, you blew it roughly out.

After you auctioned a walk-on part in your poems,
I blew you, charitably, on my knees, in luxury seclusion –
but held you at arm's length for months: missed calls,
smutty voicemails, stained tie. 'Til I rolled over, speechless.

Here I am on my back, a part in your risible poems,
Brazilian Sonnets. One is 'wooed, but unwon', 'tough as
election promises', 'heartless by the' alliterative 'hearth'.

I'm here just to rip my briefs off. But that fantasy bridge
and the NHS windfall were my ideas! So is tying you up
with your filthy tie for real grief from real party whips.

If thou must love me, let it be for nought

One night a week is not enough, naughty man,
under these conditions! Re-negotiate! That
screaming is your bastard, you libertarian bore.
She's my day job. *You* get up in the night; fair deal.

If you trade on, it won't be with the Chinese.
Don't say: Belgium is too far across the water.
One trades best with those who are near. I'm near,
discomforting allegory for your post-Brexit ambition.

Love me like you do power, which is so near, you say;
or I'll lose the power to love you, *bonito!* I'll play
the bossa nova while you do *this* boss a favour, the wimp
of Wimpole St. cleaning the bowl with your tongue.

Then you'll play Britain and I'll play Europe:
fuck me as much as you like, I'll not come.

I never gave a lock of hair away

Never gave a thing away to a man
'til I met you, *bonito*, kept thoughts
to myself, and men kept hands to themselves.
No Full Brazilian selfie for your Brazilian sonnet!

Wasn't born yesterday. Crinkles and wrinkles shape
my weekly money column: *Recipes for a Cake
and Eat it Britain.* You confuse Lebanon-Libya,
Bermuda-Barbados, 'til I comb out your careless kinks.

Call me Mistress Elizabeth! Over the bowl, Flush!
Take a Hard Brexit strapping on your pale doggie cheeks!
Weep in spotty canine latex, your blonde topknot peeping!

I take your photograph. Let's call it a *safey* –
insurance in a locked drawer at my mother's. It'll
give your vaulting career my drooping kiss of death.

The soul's Rialto hath its merchandise

My little piggy goes to the free market. You say:
'The fundamental unit of post-Brexit trade
will be American Boneless Pork Recta!'
Low in the water container ships chug to port.

Your counterpart Pandar ponderously opens
his ministerial box: all Pandemonium breaks loose.
He solicits the State Bard to pen a panegyric,
panglossic optimism for Independence Day.

Alone, we exchange bodily fluids, *bonito*. Sex
peddles uphill, as on a Boris bike: purple cheeks,
fish-breath, rough kisses: porcine quickie.

This polar-white strand I pick from the pillow
I'll send for analysis, paternalistic bonus in perpetuity,
as you cool and drift into soft Brexchosis.

A heavy heart, Belovèd, have I borne

Your sleep-talk's threaded like a string of pearls
shuffling to the samba of your ambition: 'We've
a bigger diaspora, *bonita*, than any other rich nation
since the autarkic 1950s of spam and liver and *triste*.

Note the eye-popping things Brits do in Brazil! Un-
British spasms of bad manners, Bo-Peep protests, V-
signs from the cliffs, the genius of our Ice Age union…'

Wake up! You bid me shake you before dawn,
arouse your deep becoming. Revive your fatty pump!
Lift yourself from your light dream (*my* nightmare:
I'm a mourning Remoaner). Face your unaccomplished fate.

The speech I sketched for you, unbelieving Leaver, is ready.
It slips onto your sincere inauthenticity like a ruptured condom.
Dead stars wink around our interminably darkening globe.

I lived with visions for my company

Lived in my head with Churchill and Thatcher,
their biographies my guide, their speeches my gospel.
On the cliffs at Roedean, sang 'Jerusalem', my soul
a truer blue (I thought) than the sea or sky before me;

though I clutched a fading ribbon, at last a blue rag.
Then you came, told me I'd still be beautiful in
the morning, when you'd be merely sober. One thrilled
at such allusion. God's Gift to me (and to all the others).

Soon learnt your private passion held no public compassion.
Chose the satisfaction of your wit, ignored
the shame of your spite, our non-disclosure agreement.

Neither socialite nor socialist (though I am an economist
and can see what's coming), I'm not for turning, at last.
You will exit my life, and I will remain in it (and the flat).

Cake and Eat It Britain

> But I must secretly forbid myself a delay of even two seconds
> with this Brazilian lady, or whatever she might be; for I may
> waste neither space nor time.
> —Robert Walser

My letters! all dead paper,… mute and white!

These papers speak the language of hush,
the dead letter of the NDA you signed
with tremulous hand, in exchange for DNA
and certain digital files. Don't speak, madam!

Listen! He said *this* and *that*. No matter. You get
Wimpole St, a golden handshake, a gold bowl for Flush,
even the Elis Regina vinyl, it's all here. But redaction's
total: these sonnets will be written over. OK? Done.

Imagine if Dox could negotiate this fast with Barnier!
Fox fixes a day in Spring to strike arms deals with the Saudis.
Go's future thunders in your past relations. Thus far

your words have ill availed. In your next article
tell how people are now pronouncing it *Bregsit*.
Normalise this madness. Mute and write.

The first time that the sun rose on thine oath

The last time austere promises are advertised
on the side of the rusty bus there will be no tickets.
Darwinian celebrities will rise from its wreckage,
scrub up into aphoristic hubris, blow

a few farty phrases on stolen trumpets. Slacken
the bonds of dependency in despondency:
moral hazard is no fickle fact but lasting truth.
Quick fixes quickly unfix; only duty endures.

Etc, etc. At one stroke, fiddle and diddle.
I'm keeping out of this one. It's all too clear
how I'm going to end up in this giggle economy.

It's not the jokes you tell, it's the jokes you know
that matter. I solemnly promise to be grim
for the sake of the future. That leaves me in stitches.

YES, call me by my pet-name!

Pet! Petsy? Petronella? Petrarca! Where Petrarch dwells
there lies Poesy, as he makes for himself a self
in language, however embarrassing his cowpat lyricism,
since he – *I* – could not hope for imperial laurels.

I'll almost miss the barked command, the Skripal panic.
Unreconciled, I'll not spend more time with my families!
She no longer calls. I sit silent with my nut-brown beer,
while she calls Go, yes, calls Go! *Ba!* I'll let it go. But

my mouth bears the testimony of those exanimate,
buried beneath my jokes, who laughed themselves
to death. East and West divide; Europe unites.
Putin turns off, and on, the gas (or whatever it is).

Don't call me Fuckface or Gruffnuts, but call me now! Or,
Petal, you'll hear the last of me, hoisted by my own pettitoes.

If I leave all for thee, wilt thou exchange

What do you mean *if* we leave? The plebiscite
was absolute. No careless talk can now exchange
the blessed result. A new range of goods from the far
Far East will complement the offal and the off-cuts.

National death comes with international debt,
the Barrett estate in the west West Indies forfeit.
There will never be another home with such dividends.
Elope to Vaucluse with the dog, paddle in Petrarch's pool!

If communal grief is transmitted epigenetically,
like slavery's, this grief could last months, dead
dead eyes gawping at trauma they can't comprehend.

These sonnets used to be funny but Ken Dodd's dad's *god*'s
dead. Can happiness be transmitted? We used to laugh at lines
like 'the wet wet wings of thy dove'. Whoever we were.

First time he kissed me, he but only kissed

Second time looks like assault to me: sprained wrist,
unable to write your column on frictionless border trade,
or wear the ring he bought you (you still have it?)
to buy your first silence, clean and white, unlike the bruise.

The third assault he landed punches (photo evidence, no?)
on your forehead. Later, his 'jism of love' (his phrase)
was delivered to your unconscious crown, tangled hair
(no samples, I assume?). Next time he held his purple thing

to your lips, unconsented, said, 'At last, you're mine!'
Trouble is, you signed off on that NDA,
unlike your *#me too* half-sisters. Don't speak, madam!

You think you're manipulative and no victim.
There are traceless nerve agents and smart delivery systems.
Spit out his effluent but swallow your pride.

Oh yes! they love through all this world of ours!

Oh no! They hate throughout their administered world.
In truth, they have corrupted power, not it them; it's
turned from a youthful string of light into a possession,
a thing to guard other things, thingy things like wealth.

Here's another thing: they lie about Muslims and Jews,
pitch race against race, hashtag Vote Leave. Whatever
they possess, it's the rest of us who're leaving it. Ask Petrarch:
'If my remain was vain, let my leave heave dividends!'

Try a Hitler gag. (They never bomb.) Or crack a joke:
*The Giant Albion was brushing his teeth in the shower
when he slipped on smooth soap and cracked his nuts! 'What
is this thing – called love?' he asked, looking at his thing.*

Every abstract noun rests upon a thing that cracks it.
I do want to sing of love, but in *this* poem it's too late.

'My future will not copy fair my past' –/ I wrote that once

'I'll be through these hapless sonnets before we hit the worst' –
I wrote that, while Go, angelic Minister of Justice,
was still spiking appeals – wrong face, wrong bonnet –
before he was shuffled onto those 'permissive bridal paths',

fences impearled with natural oils from budding tools,
fast comforts of the dogging sites of Global Britain.
Leave here the voice I borrowed to Easter-parade in,
and let me write their future's epitaph:

They've got their country back for 'us'; now they want us
for themselves, so the Nation will be theirs forever,
'Greensleeves' piped around the American mall as we
zero-hour the trolleys of offal we can't stomach or afford.

We must stay frosty as Laura on Good Friday, spit back
at pauperising Maundy monarchs. *You* know that.

       (for James Byrne)
Easter 2018

January–March 2018

Acknowledgements

Some of these poems were published in my pamphlets *Petrarch 3* (Crater 36), Crater Press, 2017, and *Hap: Understudies of Thomas Wyatt's Petrarch*, Knives Forks and Spoons, 2018.

Poems appeared in the following magazines: *Anthropocene, Blackbox Manifold, Blaze Vox, Card Alpha, Cumulus, International Times, Molly Bloom, Pages, Poetry at Sangam, Poetry Wales, A Restricted View from Under the Hedge, Shearsman, Smithereens, Some Roast Poet, Stride, Tears in the Fence,* and *The Wolf.*

Others appeared in the anthologies: *Face Down in the Book of Revelations: Peter Hughes at 60.* ed. Lynne Hughes, Oystercatcher/Sea-pie, 2016; *Badge of Shame, Purge 5: a strong and stable production,* ed. Robert Hampson, Pushtika, 2017; *For Robert: An Anthology,* ed. Del Olsen, RHU Poetics Research Centre/Crinoline Editions, June 2017; *The Other Room Anthology 10,* eds. James Davies, Tom Jenks, Scott Thurston, 2018.

A sample of these poems will be found in *The Robert Sheppard Companion,* eds. James Byrne and Christopher Madden, Shearsman Books, 2019.

Some poems appear illustratively in my essay 'Era il giorno ch'al sol si scoloraro': A derivative dérive into/out of Petrarch's Sonnet 3', in editor Carole Birkan-Berz's *Translating Petrarch's Poetry.* Legenda, 2020.

'Useless Landscape' was commissioned for the 'Myths of the Modern Woman' afternoon at Bluecoat, Liverpool, 2016, and was published in a booklet to accompany the second showing of Melissa Gordon's Mina Loy installation, 'Collision', in 2018.

'Meaning Me' is displayed on the wall of the Belvedere public house, Liverpool.

Thanks to all the editors, curators, activists and enthusiasts who first published these works.

Excerpts from a letter by Lee Harwood © Estate of Lee Harwood.

Note

The starter for 'Petrarch 3', 'That pitiful morning…', I wrote as a crib translation for use in a chapter on the Petrarch variations of Peter Hughes and Tim Atkins in my critical work *The Meaning of Form in Contemporary Innovative Poetry* but, enraptured by the versioning bug, I was off on one, with the procedures of the other dedicatees of the poems, Harry Mathews' 'Trial Impressions' and Nicholas Moore's *Spleen*, in mind. My essay 'Era il giorno ch'al sol si scoloraro': A derivative dérive into/out of Petrarch's Sonnet 3' is an account of their writing, in which I detail some of the non-Petrarchan borrowings (the French symbolists for example) and trace how the more the sequence became deliberately derivative the more it took on the aspects of a dérive.

Similarly, most of the poems that follow are variations or transpositions of poems by Milton, Wyatt, Surrey, Charlotte Smith and Elizabeth Barrett Browning. In the case of Wyatt completely and Surrey (in 'The Unfortunate Traveller') and Smith (in 'Petrarch of Petworth'), I have concentrated on *their* versions of Petrarch's sonnets, sometimes the same ones. I believe I have signposted, either directly in titles, or through particular quotation in titles, the source poems; editions consulted are listed in the resources below. All the poems are canonical, although Charlotte Smith (my fellow Sussex poet) is less known. In her case, I have extended my practice of quoting one selected poem by the poet at the head of each set of this book to two.

The two poems for Lee Harwood, and the sequences 'It's Nothing' and 'Breakout', are not variations in the same way.

The English Strain is the first book of a trilogy. Book two, which consists of transpositions of the sonnets of the Renaissance poet Michael Drayton, appears as *Bad Idea* (published by Knives, Forks and Spoons, 2021). The third part of the project is entitled *British Standards* and consists of versions of various Romantic-era sonnets.

The cover image is by Patricia Farrell and features the features of Petrarch, Wyatt, Surrey, Smith and Browning.

Selected Resources

Atkins, Tim. *Collected Petrarch*. London: Crater, 2014.
Baudelaire, Charles. trans. Jeffrey Wagner, *Selected Poems*. London: Panther, 1971.
Brigden, Susan. *Thomas Wyatt: The Heart's Forest*. London: Faber and Faber, 2012.
Browning, Elizabeth Barrett. *Aurora Leigh*. London: The Women's Press, 1978.
Browning, Elizabeth Barrett. *The Poetical Works of Elizabeth Barrett Browning*. London, Edinburgh, etc: Henry Frowde, 1904.
Browning, R. and E.B. *The Letters of Robert Browning and Elizabeth Barrett Browning*. London: John Murray, 1913.
Childs, Jessie. *Henry VIII's Last Victim: The Life and Times of Henry Howard, Earl of Surrey*. New York, NY: Thomas Dunne Books, 2007.
Forster, Margaret. *Elizabeth Barrett Browning*. London: Vintage, 1998.
Hughes, Peter. *Quite Frankly: After Petrarch's Sonnets*. Hastings: Reality Street Editions, 2015.
Johnson, Boris. 'Brexit Speech', at blogs.spectator.co.uk/2018/02/full-text-boris-johnsons-brexit-speech (accessed February 19th February 2018).
Keene, Dennis. ed. *Henry Howard, Earl of Surrey: Selected Poems*. Manchester: Carcanet Press, 1985.
Mathews, Harry. *A Mid-Season Sky: Poems 1954-1991*. Manchester: Carcanet Press, 1992.
Milton, John. *Poetical Works*. London and Oxford: Oxford University Press, 1969.
Moore, Nicholas. *Spleen*. London: Menard Press, 1990.
Muir, Kenneth. ed. *Sir Thomas Wyatt: The Collected Poems*. London: Routledge and Kegan Paul, 1949.
Nash, Thomas. *The Unfortunate Traveller, or The Life of Jacke Wilton*. London: John Lehmann, 1948.
Petrarch, Francesco. trans., Mark Musa, *Selections from the Canzoniere and Other Works*. Oxford and New York, NY: Oxford University Press, 1985.
Petrarch, Francesco. *Canzoniere*, poem 3, at petrarch.petersadlon.com/canzoniere.html?poem=3 (accessed 7 May 2014).
Rebholtz, R.A. ed. *Sir Thomas Wyatt: The Complete Poems* Harmonds-worth: Penguin, 1978.
Rimbaud, Arthur. trans., Paul Schmidt, *Complete Works*. New York, NY and London, etc: Harper Perennial, 2008.

Sheppard, Robert. 'Robert Sheppard on the Petrarch Boys', at robertsheppard.blogspot.co.uk/2013/12/robert-sheppard-on-petrarch-boys-peter.html (accessed 29 June 2014).
Sheppard, Robert. *A Translated Man.* Bristol: Shearsman Books, 2013.
Sheppard, Robert. *The Meaning of Form in Contemporary Innovative Poetry.* New York, NY: Palgrave, 2016.
Sheppard, Robert. 'Era il giorno ch'al sol si scoloraro': A derivative dérive into/out of Petrarch's Sonnet 3', in ed. Carole Birkan-Berz. *Translating Petrarch's Poetry.* Oxford: Legenda, 2020.
Shulman, Nicola. *Graven with Diamonds: The Many Lives of Thomas Wyatt.* London: Short Books, 2011.
Spiller, Michael. *Early Modern Sonneteers: from Wyatt to Milton.* Tavistock: Northcote House, 2001.
Curran, Stuart. ed. *The Poems of Charlotte Smith.* Oxford and New York, NY: Oxford University Press, 1993.
Themerson, Stefan. *Bayamus and the Theatre of Semantic Poetry.* London: Gaberbocchus Press, 1965.
Thomson, Patricia. *Sir Thomas Wyatt and His Background.* Palo Alto, CA: Stanford University Press, 1964.
Verlaine, Paul. trans. Martin Sorrell. *Selected Poems.* Oxford and New York, NY: Oxford University Press, 1999.
Walser, Robert. trans. Christopher Middleton and others. *The Walk and other stories.* London: Serpent's Tail, 2013.
Woolf, Virginia. *Flush.* London: Vintage, 2002.

www.ingramcontent.com/pod-product-compliance
Lightning Source LLC
Chambersburg PA
CBHW031152160426
43193CB00008B/341